KEYS OF POWER

From Tears to Triumph

Book 1

Also by Qumran Taj C.P.C.

Tarot Cards: A Reader's Workbook

KEYS OF POWER

From Tears to Triumph

Book 1

QUMRAN TAJ C.P.C.

Crown Prince Publications

Long Island, New York - CrownPrincePublications.com

Copyright © 2017 Qumran Taj
All rights reserved. This book or parts thereof may not be reproduced in any form, stored in any retrieval system in any form, or transmitted in any form by any means- electronic, mechanical, photocopy, recording, or otherwise-without prior written permission of the publisher, except as provided by the United States of America copyright law.

ISBN: 978-0-692-03401-9

All photographs and illustrations used in this book are copyright free and altered by permission of their providers. No attributions are required. All graphics are for illustrative purposes only.

DEDICATION

To my father. It was by his hand that I first came to know the great spiritual masters, faith, and God. At last, I have grasped the divine providence in the circumstances of my birth. For that I am eternally grateful.

ACKNOWLEDGMENTS

With much gratitude I acknowledge the following individuals without which this publication would not have seen the light of day.

Cathy Maury. What can I say about a woman that believes in me despite all evidence to the contrary? The value of her sage advice cannot be overstated. She has earned my undying love and loyalty.

Peter Moray, my editor extraordinaire. He is ever a source of wisdom and inspiration to me. Professionally speaking, he is a rare commodity. Thanks Pete!

CONTENTS

1	Are You Troubled?	1
2	Don't Believe Me!	5
3	Failure Is Feedback	11
4	Power Here And Now	17
5	Program Beliefs	25
6	Sensory Deception	33
7	The Face In The Mirror	41
8	The Time Bomb	47
9	Let's Get Practical	55
10	Hard Way vs Easy Way	63
11	The Ring Of Truth	67
12	Mr. Play-Doh	73
13	The Tool Box	81
14	The Crown	95
	About The Author	

Chapter 1

ARE YOU TROUBLED?

This is your moment of truth, that instant when you decide if reading this page is worth the investment. As an author I want you to read my book, but to be perfectly honest, what you paid for it won't make much difference in my life financially. What DOES matter to me is touching the life of someone who is now today as I myself was many years ago. If I can help you to be wealthy, healthy and happy, in some way your success can be my success or at least the success I would have enjoyed myself much earlier in life had I the occasion to read the book you now hold in your hands.

Are you troubled? Have you fallen into a pit of despair or are you one of those souls who has lost hope that your dreams will come true? Have you given up on happiness in this lifetime? Is there some obstacle in your life that has persisted despite all your efforts to remove it? Have the various circumstances in your experience made you feel like a failure? If your answer to any of these questions is yes, then this book is written for you.

I don't believe in coincidence. In my view, things happen because something causes them to. What caused you to be here now, reading these words? We may never know the answer to that question, but since we have found each other, let's think about your personal life journey.

Each of us is on a journey. We know how, when and where it began, but we do not know how or when it will end. While we are taking this tour of life we want to experience good things along the way. Who doesn't want peace, prosperity, health, fulfillment, and the love and respect of the people who matter most to us?

The American poet and educator, Henry Wadsworth Longfellow, wrote: "Into each life, some rain must fall." It's safe to say that most of us expect "some rain" in our travels. What we don't expect are endless torrential downpours, earthquakes, and tsunamis! There are a great many individuals out there that are convinced life stacked the deck against them from the start. Do you feel like no matter what you do your efforts end in frustration and failure? This feeling can be like a great weight around the neck of someone desperately trying to tread water after their ship sank into the ocean.

These chapters are not a collection of inspirational maxims. They are tools of the most practical kind. Without danger of hyperbole it can truthfully be said that the concepts, counsel, and philosophies in this little book can literally turn tears into triumph. Let us be perfectly clear on this point: No matter what your life is like today, the power to change is present within you here and now. The extent of your transformation is entirely up to you. Every individual is a world unto themselves. No two lives are exactly the same, no two people have the same needs. Take the parts of this message that resonate with you and leave the rest behind.

These pages have one purpose and one purpose only: to help you get from here to there. 'Here' is wherever you don't want to be, wherever you need to leave -- a bad relationship, a job where you're not appreciated, self-destructive behavior, unhappiness, and suffering. 'There' is wherever you most desire to be, but have not (yet) found a way to.

A journey is a collection of starts, stops, twists, turns, crossroads, and lots of choices. You've read this far and now you arrive at the first crossroads and a new choice to make. Will you continue reading? If you answer yes, the road from here on departs from the life course you've taken up until now. Growth and personal empowerment are ahead on this new course. On the other hand, if you answer no, I suspect your life will continue as before. Only you can decide if that's a good thing.

For those that decide to read on, welcome to an exhilarating life of self-discovery, self-empowerment and the freedom to be who and what you truly are! To you alone are granted the Keys of Power.

QUMRAN TAJ

Chapter 2

DON'T BELIEVE ME!

My father deserves full credit for turning me on to the glories of reading. Some of the books I read as a young boy so captured my heart that they influence my personal evolution to this very day. Some of the people I "met" in these volumes had spiritual gifts, powerful gifts, that I could only dream about in those early days. At that time, I accepted the accounts of their words and deeds as any young, naive reader might. Still, even then there were nagging doubts. What if these people were no more than fictional characters created to sell books? What if the things my favorite characters "did" were merely tall tales one reads to a child at bedtime? An intense fire burned brightly inside me. I had to know for sure if these extraordinary spiritual powers were fact or fiction.

In the end, it became clear that reading a story about what someone else did can be a great inspiration, but there was no way for me to know for sure if what I was reading was truth or a fairy tale. There was only one way to extinguish those nagging doubts. I had to perform some impossible feat of spiritual mastery. This was no small task for a boy barely out of single digits.

At this stage in my life, I have not yet mastered all the secrets of the great adepts, but my being able to duplicate some of their feats (many times over) confirmed to me without a shadow of a doubt that such things are indeed possible. It also assured me that the books I had read in my youth contained a certain core truth. At last, I knew for sure that my "heroes" were real flesh and blood humans like me or, at very least, that the stories were based on real people who actually lived and who could accomplish wondrous things!

My policy is to refrain from relating my own accomplishments in the more mystical vein. It is unlikely you would believe me anyhow, so why bother? Instead, allow me to pose a few questions and see how they strike you, shall we?

Suppose I told you that I could command the weather to change dramatically or alter the course of a raging hurricane. Would you believe me? If I told you that I could see through the human body of someone who was 1,000 miles away from me, a perfect stranger, and relate intimate details about specific physical ailments they had, would you believe me? Let's try one more. Suppose someone told you that as my client they had requested me to use some of my "magic," as they called it, to cause a complex series of specific events to occur for them in connection with a 3rd individual? Would you believe any of this simply because I told you so in my book?

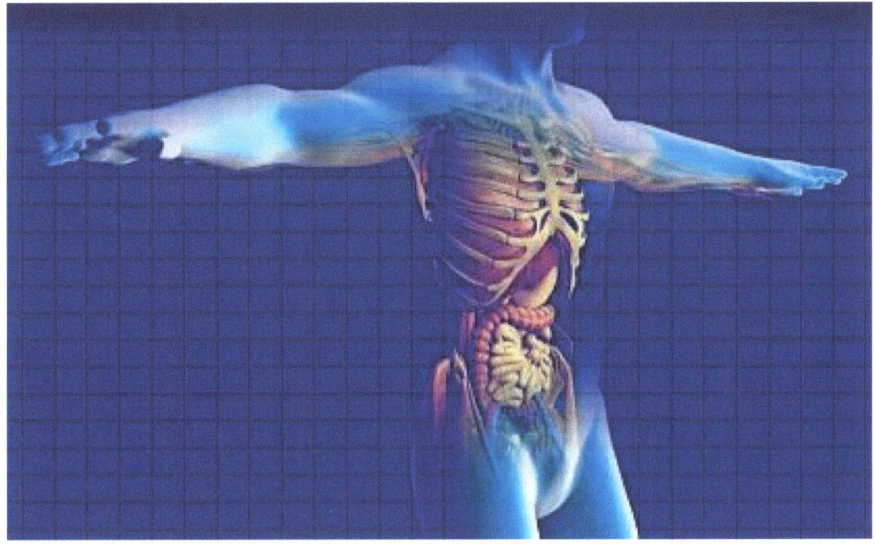

If you answered "no" to the question "would you believe me?," then you understand my dilemma all those years ago. I wanted to believe the stories, but how could I put faith in an author I didn't know who wrote about people, places, and events I was equally ignorant of? My rational mind could not bring itself to believe these tales without further corroboration and proof.

For this reason, I say DON'T BELIEVE ME! Instead, if you prefer, follow my example of years ago and prove these teachings to yourself. Then, and only then, will you truly know that my words are worthy of your trust. On the other hand, for those of you who dare to believe and accept these truths at face value, you will not be disappointed.

Yes, you *ARE* powerful but this book is not about doing miraculous works. It is about reaching your goals and dreams.

With all this talk of miraculous accomplishments and spiritual masters, it is important that you understand one thing clearly: This book is NOT about doing powerful works for their own sake. In fact, this book is not about spiritual masters, psychic gifts or paranormal phenomena of any kind. The examples cited above are here only to drive home a fundamental point about humanity and it is this: a human being is far, FAR more powerful than the average person is ever led to believe. YOU are far greater than you have ever imagined. In other words, making significant, mundane changes in your circumstances, relationships, and personal advancement is light stuff compared to the amazing things we are all capable of.

Changing your life, or aspects of it, does not require that you learn to control nature in fantastical ways or perform miracles! Far from it. What it does require is a willingness on your part to take a fresh look at who and what you believe yourself to be and what you are capable of accomplishing. Reexamining your thoughts, emotions and belief system will produce wonderful insights that will profoundly change how you feel about yourself and the world around you.

QUMRAN TAJ

Chapter 3

FAILURE IS FEEDBACK

We can and should usually substitute the word feedback in place of the word failure. The word failure makes us feel bad about ourselves. It also has the distinction of being an inappropriate and inaccurate way to describe an event where the result we get is not the one we want. If we stop using that word the way it is normally applied to people, we are not being overly sensitive, we are being more intelligent. People tend to identify the word failure with something they ARE instead of something they DID. That can be a fatal flaw.

After a series of so-called failures, we may begin to feel as though we are failures as human beings instead of seeing individual failures as part of a feedback loop that provides us with data we can use to achieve success. Ironically, we as a society hold failure in such utter contempt that we overlook the lessons it has in store for us. Every so-called "failure" carries within it the seeds of a greater success.

Countless highly successful people have discovered the gold mine in what the common man ignorantly discards as a worthless experience he would rather forget.

What follows are a few words from individuals that have succeeded on a spectacular scale. Curiously enough, the highly successful are, more often than not, also experts on failure. Why so? Because these individuals are well acquainted with failure, having done it so many times themselves. What separates them from people who try but never achieve their goals may very well be their attitude AFTER they fail.

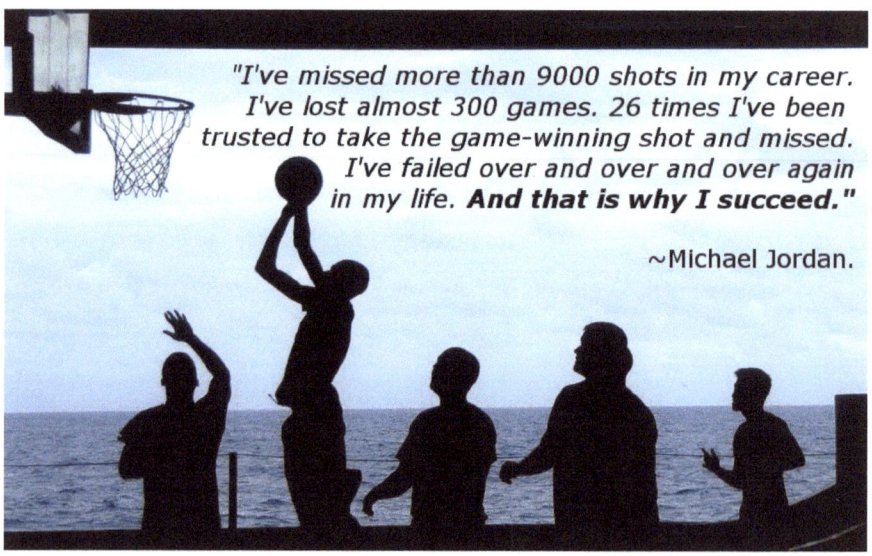

"I've missed more than 9000 shots in my career. I've lost almost 300 games. 26 times I've been trusted to take the game-winning shot and missed. I've failed over and over and over again in my life. **And that is why I succeed.**"

~Michael Jordan.

"Failure should be our teacher, not our undertaker. Failure is a delay, not defeat. It is a temporary detour, not a dead-end. Failure is something we can avoid only by saying nothing, doing nothing, and being nothing." ~Denis Waitley

"Success represents the 1% of your work which results from the 99% that is called failure."
~Soichiro Honda

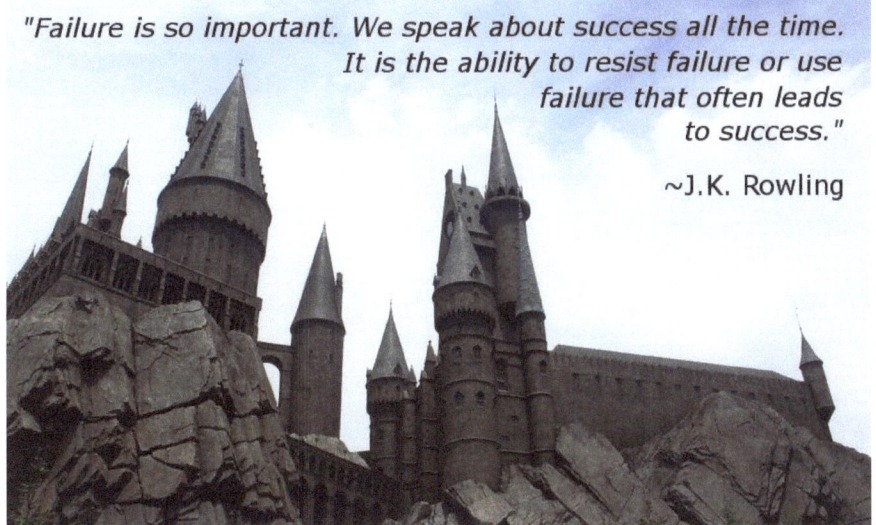

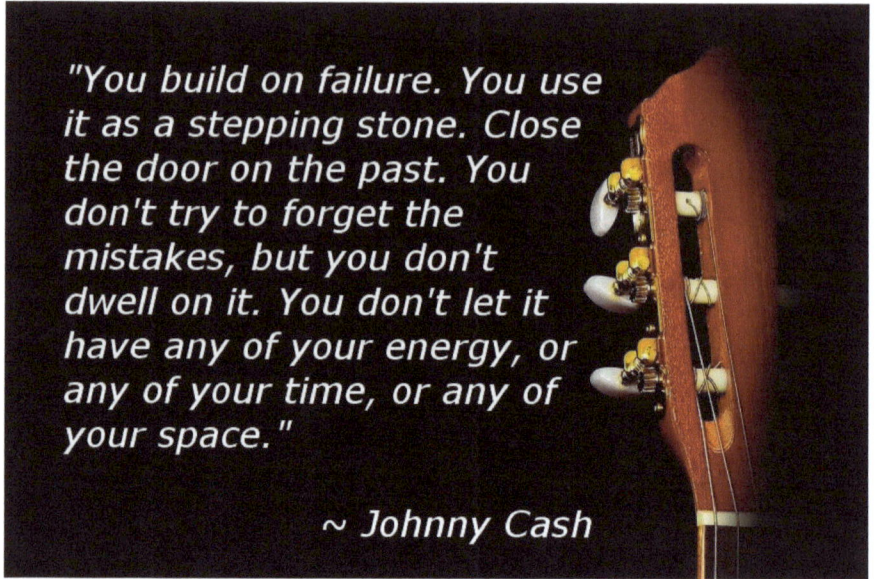

"You build on failure. You use it as a stepping stone. Close the door on the past. You don't try to forget the mistakes, but you don't dwell on it. You don't let it have any of your energy, or any of your time, or any of your space."

~ Johnny Cash

Fortunately, we each live in a continuous feedback loop. Our world functions as a kind of cause and effect, action and reaction machine. We get this action/reaction feedback all day, every day. It can help us gauge how successful our individual viewpoints are. We can choose to either ignore the loop, as most people do, or we can learn from it. The lives of the individuals quoted in this chapter indicate what can happen when we mine the rich feedback data that is erroneously called "failure" in our society.

Action and Reaction

Everything we do, say, think or feel qualifies as an action. In case you're wondering why intangible thoughts and emotions are also considered actions in this context, it is simply because virtually every tangible thing you do is preceded by an intangible thought, emotion or some combination of the two. Our beliefs color everything we think, feel, and consequently, they influence every action we take or fail to take. Logically it follows that, in order to alter the results we get in life, in order to experience the joy of achieving true and lasting success (whatever "success" means to you personally), you must go to the root cause of your actions: your beliefs, your thoughts, and your feelings.

Most readers will have no trouble understanding the correlation between beliefs, thoughts, emotions, actions and results. In the real world, however, knowing what we should do is one thing, but DOING what we should do is quite another. Our handy-dandy graphic doesn't help us with the latter. Fortunately, there are ways and means at your disposal to create successful habits.

Having said that, there is something to be said for doing whatever you want and taking what can be called the "organic" path to change. The "organic" path is not as healthy as one might hope. This course of action lets you suffer the consequences of horrible choices and, eventually, you might decide it is more painful to do the wrong thing than to do what your intelligence said you should have done in the first place - provided, of course, that you survive your own horrible choices.

Ultimately, we have the right to our thoughts, feelings, beliefs and the freedom to choose. As it turns out, the simple power to choose may be the greatest "super power" you have. The super aspect of it comes into play at the intangible level. Choice within the arena of the mind and emotions has vast repercussions in your mundane experience.

Choosing to regard the results of your activity as feedback instead of failure could possibly be the smartest thing you do on any given day.

Chapter 4

POWER HERE AND NOW

No matter what your life is like today, the power to change is within you here and now. Pause for a moment, if you will, to make this bold declaration in the first person. With as much confidence and conviction as you can muster say to yourself, "No matter what my life is like today, the power to change is within me here and now."

But can this really be true? Some of you will believe the answer is obvious. Quickly you'll answer, "No!" I am here to tell you that it is indeed true. You have the power to transform the conditions and circumstances in your life in ways you probably never imagined possible before. These words are true, but you don't have to take my word for it, you will soon be shown ways to prove these things to yourself.

What is your most pressing need? What is most important

to you? Don't answer what is important to your spouse or to your employer or to your family. What is most important to YOU? What are your biggest life challenges? What are you most afraid of? With a sense of critical need, the possibility of not getting what you're desperate for often inspires fear.

Become a 'Fear-breathing' Dragonslayer!

How easy it is for me to advise you to face down your greatest fears when I sit here in the lap of comfort and security, fingers happily typing away! Granted, there's nothing easier than for a stranger to tell you to be brave when terror grabs hold of your heart and squeezes! As someone thoroughly familiar with that dreadful feeling, someone who spent half a lifetime imprisoned by fear, allow me to share something that might help the next time you're in the grip of terror or paralyzed by severe nervousness.

It may sound a little counter-intuitive, but I recommend that you embrace the fear and hold it as close as you can. Savor it. Be present with it. Slurp it up like hot soup! Don't run from fear or it will chase you like a predator. Instead, look it straight in the eye and see it for what it is, an emotional reaction. Nothing less, nothing more. Like love, hate, or jealousy, fear exists inside you. Fear is your creation, your "fear-breathing dragon," your "monster" under the bed. It won't kill you. It won't even hurt you. In fact, oddly enough, face it head on, stand toe-to-toe with the "dragons" you fear and one by one they will wither and die. Seek out your fears, revisit them often and slay them without mercy.

Naturally, if you are in danger, you must find safety. Danger can hurt you. Fear, on the other hand, is powerless without your complicity. Fear has only one chance to harm you. It must somehow make you retreat when you should step forward, stay silent when you should speak out, think you are weak when you are strong and believe more in what you see outside than in what you are inside. The bottom line here is that fear has only one mortal enemy, only one thing fear itself must fear, and that thing is YOU.

What Is Success?

On a related subject, what does the word "success" mean to you personally? Success means something different to each individual. What would life look like if you were the person you want to be? How would your life be different than it is today? Would you look, speak, feel or think differently? Maybe you want more money, better health, more time to spend with family and friends, more and better vacations, to own your own house, or to change your career?

What would your typical day look like if you could make it anything you want? What if you had the power at this very moment to reformat your life or those parts of it that are most important to you?

The Keys Of Power materials will clearly explain how to direct the awesome power within to do just that. Does this sound too good to be true? The truth is we have been conditioned by society to believe that happiness is beyond our reach. We are told we have the right to the pursuit of happiness but not the right to BE happy! Society has taught us that we must be "lucky" in order for us to live "the good life." Yet nothing could be further from the truth! Here is the truth, plain and simple:

A man (or woman) in his right domain, being aware of who and what he is, is master of his domain. No, not "master" as in being a tyrant. To the contrary, he or she works in harmony with the creative force within which we all have our being. This creative power, this divine essence, I AM allows events, circumstances and other people to flow naturally into the scenario you have created within. You may not yet be able to agree with the truth as stated here, but in time you will grasp its true meaning. This realization will usher in wonderful developments in your life.

Those who know me personally know that my life has been spent looking for what makes this world tick behind the scenes. Along the way, I've studied or examined countless theories, beliefs, doctrines, religions, New Age thought, quantum physics, metaphysics, the occult and the list goes on.

Not so long ago, it finally dawned on me that all of these branches of knowledge share something in common. They have a common core and a common source of power. We all do. Personally, I take no credit for discovering anything. This truth has been known since before time began. Nevertheless, when I took hold of this knowledge it transformed my life. In turn, if you do likewise it cannot fail to transform your life in ways that are important to you.

This story begins and ends with a simple statement:

I AM that I AM

Many people know this phrase. It is from the Bible at Exodus 3:14.

Having cited Bible scripture, it is an ideal time to make one thing crystal clear: This book is not religious in any conventional way and I will never promote any religion whatsoever. This policy does not intend to cast aspersions on religious faith. It simply is not the purpose of the Keys Of Power series to address itself to doctrinal, religious dogma. As mentioned earlier, our focus is on universal truths that are more ancient than religion. Virtually every religion has appropriated bits and parts of this universal truth and inserted it into their teachings as it suited their purposes. For this reason, when I use words like "God" or "spirit" or "divinity" some people will automatically interpret them religiously. This is NOT the sense in which these words are used in my work. This is why atheists can gain the very same benefit from this material as the most devout followers of their religion of choice. No offense or disrespect is intended to devotees of any faith. Having been a devout Christian for many years I am sensitive to believers. I am also sensitive to those individuals who see a wonderful spiritual universe devoid of religious bias.

You see, "I AM" is a universal truth so, as you might imagine, this truth, this concept can be found throughout the world's greatest literature, the words of poets, philosophers, religious holy books and many non-religious sources as well. You can call truth by any name you prefer, dress it up in the "clothing" and trappings that appeal to you best, but the truth remains truth.

The expression "I AM" is a declaration of BEING. It is your true identity, your true Self. I AM speaks to the consciousness, the awareness of who and what you really are behind the facade of skin and bones. I confess that at first glance all this talk of "I AM" and "I AM That I AM" struck me as nothing more than semantic nonsense. What possible advantage could awareness of "BEING" be to me? How does all of this help me cope with my laundry list of daily challenges?

This is where that old expression applies: "If only I knew then what I know now!" As you continue to consider these pages you will learn that realigning yourself with your "I AM," your core power, your core Self, is very practical. It has a wonderful impact on your daily living and touches every part of your mundane existence: finances, family, career, health, love - virtually every part of life.

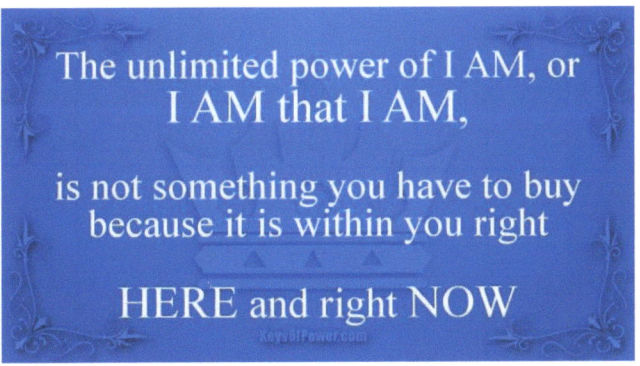

Challenges are approached in an entirely new way. You find yourself flowing through and overcoming problems with confidence and poise. Struggle and strain cease to be your default way of dealing with adversity. There will develop in you an abiding sense of being bigger than any challenge that might knock on your door. Becoming aware of the I AM in you is key to being the creative master of your domain instead of living at the mercy of every shift of the wind or the ebb and flow of the tides of circumstance.

"I AM that I AM"

Over the centuries people have obscured the knowledge of I AM. They have attached all kinds of religious doctrines, magical traditions, superstitions, do's and don'ts and taboos to the I AM, almost to the point of completely burying it in ancient history. That is why "I AM" is sometimes called the "lost word" or the "lost name of God."

Knowing the power of "I AM that I AM" is one of the Keys of Power. It is a truth that is timeless, reliable and freely available to even the most common person living in the lowliest condition in the world.

This book is the first in a series that will focus on how you can benefit in practical ways from the ONE power, the ONE awareness, the ONE consciousness that each and every human being possesses. This knowledge, if used with intelligence and intention, will align you and empower you to make the kinds of changes that are most important to you and your loved ones.

Chapter 5

PROGRAM BELIEFS

This chapter has an A-side and a B-side. The A-side is about how we are affected by the beliefs we hold to be true. The B-side ties this into "I AM," your true identity and the source of your real power.

Any belief system that does not have a positive impact on your life should be replaced by one that does. If your beliefs do not serve you, if they do not make you wealthy, healthy and happy, if the beliefs you hold to be true do not, in fact, improve the quality of your life, they should be replaced by those that do.

Your beliefs will either empower you or disempower you, help you or hinder you. Your beliefs are like a program on your computer or an app on your phone. Install the right app and it can make life sweet and easy, but bad programming can make your devices go crazy and turn your life into a living Hell.

Similarly, what you believe to be true and accurate will determine how you feel about things, how you act toward other people, how you deal with any given situation, even how you think and feel about yourself, your appearance, your intelligence, your confidence and your self-esteem. Whatever you believe about your life creates the life you believe in.

Here's a question for you: Do you believe that your opinions about who and what you are, your relationships, your community, your opinions about religion, politics, race relations, sex, human rights, are supported by solid facts and reliable information? That question answers itself, doesn't it?

ALL of us imagine that our opinions are supported, at least partially, by accurate information. Otherwise, how could we believe it? The thing is, the world is full of people with very different beliefs who are just as convinced as you are that their viewpoints are also supported by facts. Do you think that these people are misinformed, ignorant, deluded or just plain stupid?

We humans tend to take notice of factoids that support our version of the truth and we tend to ignore evidence that doesn't support our conclusions. It's just the way the human brain works. That's why when you ask someone to explain why they believe something, they can usually rattle off a few facts that sound on the surface of it to be logical and rational.

You see the problem with false, disempowering beliefs is that we believe them. We cling to the supporting "facts" we've gathered, no matter how sparse or irrelevant, and hold on for dear life!

But there's something else that factors into what we believe: We enjoy being RIGHT. Let's face it, it feels good to be right, don't you agree? Conversely, it generally feels bad when we discover that we are wrong about something, especially things we have believed for years. Somehow a belief we have held for a long time feels better established and more credible than a new idea. Then there is the 'saving face' aspect of human relations. Admitting to others that we are wrong can make us feel foolish, uneducated, ignorant, resentful and even embarrassed.

Now hold on to your hat because what I'm about to say next may shock you: Your beliefs do not have to be based on facts in order for them to be true for you. Let me repeat the last sentence for emphasis. Your beliefs do NOT have to be based on facts in order for them to be true for you.

This idea will be a thorn in the proverbial paw of the logical mind. Facts are the gold standard of knowledge, right? While facts are the main staple the mind loves to feed on, they often obscure the truth. What is true is what is actually REAL. For the purpose of these lessons "Truth" can be defined as "that which causes to become." In other words, a real thing is a cause that produces an effect. We won't spend much time on this concept in this section, but a simple example might satisfy those folks who won't be able to enjoy the rest of the book until they get a handle on the difference between so-called facts and truth.

Imagine someone who decides they will finally succeed at something they tried many times before - and failed to do every time. It doesn't matter what the goal is. It can be anything. You fill in the blank. Look at the "facts" in this case. This person has tried and failed at every attempt, despite continued efforts to "fix" whatever was causing said failure.

At some point, this individual decides to believe they will succeed even in the face of all evidence to the contrary. They simply find some way to bolster their confidence, focus on their strengths and disregard previous failures because they are convinced that the past is dead and gone and has no bearing on the present.

Their belief that they can win now when they have lost every time before may not be supported by facts. Statistically speaking, the odds against them may be very great. The difference in the now is that somehow this individual finds a new, more effective way to believe. A new reason and method of belief. That belief may translate to a different approach to the task at hand. Regardless of the so-called facts of the past, the result in the present is success! The first of many to come. It is a truism that success breeds success. Armed with a new and successful belief system, this person will succeed where they consistently failed before.

Who can say what changed here? Was it the mental attitude? Maybe he or she prepared for the challenge in a different way. Whatever the details, the mechanics of the win, the catalyst was a new and empowering belief that appeared "out of thin air."

Truth has power. Truth causes things to happen. Truth can be found in the most unlikely places, including fiction and fantasy. If none of this makes sense to you yet, just follow along a bit longer and facts will give way to truth as they always do.

Side "B"

The volume you read now is book one of a series that features what I call the "I AM" teachings. I AM is your true identity once you've stripped away all the qualifiers, labels and limitations people acquire for themselves. I AM is a declaration of ultimate, supreme BEING. It is the lost name of God and the true name of every sentient creature.

Earlier I quoted a text from the Bible from the book of Exodus. This is part of a famous passage wherein Moses asks God what his name is. God told Moses to declare that he would deliver the Hebrews out of slavery in Egypt. But then Moses asks God, "But what if people ask me what is God's name?" At this point in Biblical history, God had never revealed his secret name. People would simply refer to him using an impersonal title like Father, Lord or Lord God or the Nameless One. Moses, living in a world full of named gods and goddesses, was keenly aware that he did not know the personal name of his own God.

In Exodus 3:14, God answers Moses, "I AM That I AM." God continues, "This is what you are to say to the Israelites; 'I AM' has sent me to you." Then in verse 15, God continues by saying, "This is my name forever, the name you shall call me from generation to generation."

To reiterate an earlier statement, I use the Bible as a psychological, metaphysical and spiritual text, NOT a religious one. In fact, you'll find in these writings references to many other sources of wisdom irrespective of religious dogma. I have discovered that spiritual truth does not have to be attached to any religion and in fact, the universal truth of I AM, or I AM That I AM, is far bigger than any religion could possibly contain. Every human being is a truly empowered being if... IF.... you can see the connection to the greater, higher Self.

God revealed his own name as I AM. He then said that was his name forever. Quite frankly, it confused people. It might even be confusing you right now. The Jews didn't quite know what to do with God's name so they outlawed its use. No one was allowed to speak the name of God. So God came to be called everything else EXCEPT the name he chose!

The confusion happens because when it comes to the divine BEING, "God," most humans work from a flawed premise. Do you know what that premise is? People usually assume that God is OUTSIDE of them. People imagine god or goddess in a million different ways, but typically they see deity outside, above, and beyond themselves. This is a fatal flaw that literally cuts them off from their true essence, their core power and the very thing they could use to recreate their lives in the form they desire most.

I AM is your only true identity. It also happens to be the name and residence of the supreme being. At this point, your head might be spinning with possibilities (hopefully) or your ingrained belief system might be dismissing this concept as ridiculous and not worth your time. It might not jibe with the so-called facts you've accumulated to prove yourself right about the nature of God and man.

The bottom line here is that your entire life can be

upgraded with the knowledge of I AM That I AM. As our series continues, this will all be made plainly apparent.

Chapter 6

SENSORY DECEPTION

Taste, touch, smell, sight and hearing are the five physical senses we use to perceive everything around us. From the moment we are born we rely on these senses to give us information about what we call the real world.

Fortunately, humankind has devised many ways to enhance the basic senses so that we can now get a much more accurate perception of reality. We have microscopes like the one at Lawrence Berkeley National Labs in California that are so powerful they can see down to .1 nanometers. Not 1-nanometer mind you, but .1 or one tenth of one nanometer. To put that into perspective, a human hair is about 75,000 nanometers in width!

Science has confirmed that what feels like a solid, unmoving table top to your hand is actually 99.9999% empty space. What little there actually is of that table top is nothing more than infinitesimally small bundles of energy moving at near the speed of light. With our fancy new technology, we have finally corroborated what Einstein said when he told us that matter equals energy.

Let's take a stroll to the other end of the size spectrum. The famous Hubble telescope can see deep into our universe. How deep? Up to 15 BILLION light years away! Obviously, our modern tools can far outperform the basic five senses we were born with. That's not surprising since there are many creatures, fellow earthlings, whose sense organs put the human set to shame.

Most people know that sharks have a keen sense of smell. They can smell one part blood in one million parts of water. Amazingly, they can smell this from hundreds of miles away! Like they say on TV, "but wait, there's more!" It is a fact that a shark's sense of smell is thousands of times better than yours or mine, but did you know that they have a peculiar sense humans do not? They can detect tiny electrical fields given off by all living organisms that help them to locate food even when it is buried in the sand! Indeed, there are thousands of species that possess senses human beings can never hope to compete with.

The interesting thing is that our ability to perceive the world around us in a far more accurate way, thanks to technological advances, also proves something that spiritual teachers have been saying for thousands of years. The great spiritual masters have told us that our wonderful human senses have been lying to us!

Naturally, these spiritual teachings don't really sink in for most of us because our basic five senses are like a childhood friend we have trusted during our entire lives. At this point, it is extremely difficult to believe that reality is anything more than what our bodies have reported to us since birth. Despite what our brain tells us, we still believe that a table top is a solid object. It doesn't matter that our brains know that it isn't even really a material object at all but instead is an energy matrix that is nearly 100% thin air! If it feels real to the touch, then it IS real as far as most people are concerned.

Nevertheless, the more we learn the more we must gradually adjust our concept of what is real and true. Otherwise, we will go on believing in a fantasy world constructed by sensory organs that cannot be relied upon to accurately report what is real and what isn't.

Let us shift gears and consider a related but different perspective.

What if I told you that the world that you perceive as being outside of you is actually not outside of you at all?

What if I told you that the closest thing I could compare your world to is a dream like the ones you experience sleeping in your bed at night? While dreaming it all seems so real, does it not? You can feel happy, sad, good, bad, even terrified. Then, occasionally, the dream becomes so bizarre that you realize it couldn't be real and so it suddenly dawns on you that you are dreaming.

Have you ever become aware that you are dreaming but, instead of waking up, you were able to consciously control the dream while still asleep? They call that having a "lucid dream." You're still asleep and dreaming but you become aware that the entire environment around you, along with everyone in it, is all happening inside your own consciousness. In effect, you are playing all the parts and subconsciously directing all the action.

Shakespeare wrote, *"Life is but a dream within a dream."*

Now, what if I told you that you could become aware that your entire so-called real world environment is similar to a dream? What if I then told you that if you become conscious and aware of this fact, you could manipulate and direct the elements of your world as if it were a lucid dream?

This may sound like science fiction or even a little insane, but this isn't a new concept. In fact, you almost certainly have heard this stuff before in various forms:

"All that we see or seem is but a *dream within a dream.*"
~ Edgar Allen Poe

Albert Einstein said, "Reality is merely an illusion, albeit a very persistent one."

"A wise man, recognizing that life is but an illusion, does not act as if it is real." ~ The Buddha

You may accept this notion of life as an illusion or reject it. That is your privilege and your right. But the larger question is, are you ready for a true and meaningful change in your life? Of course, you could move forward with your old belief system firmly in place but ask yourself, "where have my beliefs gotten me so far?"

Please do not misunderstand me. I am not saying everyone who reads this book is having a bad life. To the contrary, I'm quite sure that some of you are having a wonderful life and are truly blessed. Other readers may also be quite happy except for a few things they would like to change. It is also quite possible that some of you are at the other end of the spectrum. Some of you may find yourselves in dire circumstances and are at a total loss as to what to do about it. You may actually have slipped into despair or even depression.

At this point, let me remind you that at the core of this "I AM" series of videos there's a simple truth. You are the I AM or the I AM that I AM of your world, of your consciousness. As such, you are fully empowered to create a far happier life than you may have thought possible before. To do that, you must become consciously aware that the circumstances you find yourself in are not outside of you and they are not beyond your control.

In order for that to happen, there must be an awakening from the dream that you call reality. Although we may not all be fully aware of it yet, the good news is that you are both the dreamer and the dream master, just like you are when you are sound asleep. Of course, your new life, or new reality if you prefer to call it that, will still be just a dream or an illusion, but it will be the dream of your choice.

As I mentioned before, you don't need to take my word for ANY of this. In fact, I much prefer that you try out what you learn here and prove it to yourself. When you experience these things for yourself you will know that what I'm telling you is completely true and accurate. Then you will know that the same laws that work for me also work for you.

Chapter 7

THE FACE IN THE MIRROR

The most common thing in the world is for one person to advise another person on the "right" way and "wrong" way of things.

The so-called "secrets" of the Keys Of Power series of books is a little like when you put your keys down somewhere and then forget where you left them. Are they really lost? Well yes, in a manner of speaking, because you don't remember where you yourself put them. Searching through the house, you eventually find them. Immediately you recall having put them there yourself!

The Keys of Power I'm always talking about are like those house keys. Technically they are lost, but when I remind you what and where they are, you'll remember you always had them. The plain truth is you always have the keys to open the doors to success.

Holodeck Dreaming

Because of the design of your body and the outward-pointing sense organs of sight, touch, taste, hearing, and smell, you have always tried to make changes in your life by controlling the outside environment around you. It is a perfectly logical and rational way to do things. You see something and you try to interact with that thing, that person or that circumstance with the tools you have used from birth. Your voice to talk and reason with people, your hands to do work, your ears and eyes to gain information and so on. Nothing could be more sensible, right?

In this first volume of the series, you saw how the five basic human senses have proven themselves to be far from complete or trustworthy. We have always imagined that our senses give us a more or less accurate report of the real world around us. In fact, our sense organs are not very good at reporting reality at all, but they are good at providing a simple frame of reference. Within this convenient frame of reference, we can learn and grow in concert with fellow humans who also perceive the razor thin range of energies that we can see, taste, smell, feel and hear.

Fans of the TV show, Star Trek, will be familiar with what is called the "Holodeck." This is short for a holographic projection room. Of course, Star Trek is fiction, as we all know, but the concept is that there was a large room aboard this spaceship that could generate an energy matrix or energy grid that would feel to the touch like a solid door, a sandy beach or the inside of an elegant jazz club of the 1940's.

Simply by manipulating these energy fields, the person on the holodeck could experience all of the sensations people are capable of. It could simulate your walking down a street, skiing the Alps or exploring a cave. Naturally, if the space ship lost power for some reason and the Holodeck stopped projecting, you would see that instead of strolling through an ancient forest, you were actually in an empty room with four walls, a floor and a ceiling.

Of course, Star Trek is fiction - for the time being anyhow. Science is quickly catching up to science fiction. The point is, our so-called real world is very much like the Holodeck on the star ship Enterprise because although our environment feels very real to the senses, the truth is that we live in an ocean of energy that is configured as our bedroom at home, our workplace, our cars, and even US! You may look into your bathroom mirror and see a familiar face staring back at you, but the reality is very different than the reflection.

Science has confirmed that what you perceive as your body, your bones, hair, skin and all the rest is actually 99.9999% empty space! What little there is of "you" is actually incredibly tiny bundles of energy circulating at near the speed of light. Now THAT is not science fiction, that is science fact.

In a sense, the person you're so familiar with, the person whose teeth you brush every morning and the body you dress every day is, in actuality, hardly even there! The same is true of everyone and everything around you.

Let's bring this all down to a practical level and see how

this knowledge benefits us.

At this point, I'm going to make a statement. Instead of asking you to believe it on my say so, I'll just ask that you accept it as a working theory for the sake of our discussion. You will soon be able to test out this working theory for yourself. Then you will know for sure that what I tell you is 100% true and accurate.

Here it is: You are a spiritual, non-physical being that exists above and beyond the mundane laws of physics, time and space. You are not the face and body you see in the mirror each morning. Rather, you are BEING itself. There are many terms for you, including Cosmic Consciousness, Awareness, and many other terms. The simplest, most accurate way to say it is simply I AM or I AM that I AM. You exist as a non-physical, non-local, non-corporeal entity while also being able to enjoy the illusion of what people erroneously call the "real world."

How NOT To Comb Your Hair

Let us illustrate it in this way. Imagine you're looking at your reflection in the mirror and decide you need a shave or your hair needs fixing. The solution is simple. You can make that happen with a brush or razor. But what if you were under the false impression that the image reflected in your mirror was the real you? What if, deluded as you are, you tried to reach out and fix the hair of the "you" in the mirror? You might try and try and try and fail again and again and again. If you continued in that way trying to manipulate that reflection, convinced as you were, that it was the real you, people would think you had lost your mind. They would be right.

Yet this is precisely what we do when we look to the outside reflection or the illusion of a real world to make the changes we want to see reflected in it. It's a little like waiting for your reflection to smile. The smile starts with you and is then reflected outwardly, not the other way around.

At this point, you have some idea of where we're going with our discussion, but there is so much more to it, so I encourage you to press on. We will be diving in deeper and learning more and more about the powerful being that you truly are and how that fact translates into recreating your life and times in your image.

QUMRAN TAJ

Chapter 8

THE TIME BOMB

The time has come to bring the "I AM" into focus and lay the foundation for making practical and powerful changes in your life.

By way of a brief recap:

1) Your five human senses distort reality.

2) Your body is 99.9999% empty space!

3) What little so-called "matter" is left is actually nothing more than unbelievably tiny clusters of energy moving at near the speed of light.

We are FAR more than we appear to be. Our sense organs tell us we're lumps of skin, bone, and blood. In reality, we are radiant beings of an energy so light and mobile that our true nature is invisible to the natural eye. One thing is certain: If you don't know who and what you are, you will not know what you are capable of doing or being. For example, if a bird believes it is a rabbit or a dog, it will never fly.

You are "a" BEING. That is to say, you are "an" awareness or pure consciousness. The last sentence is fine as far as it goes, but there is an even more accurate way to say this. You aren't merely "a being" as in the case of many beings, you are BEING as in the case of only ONE. You aren't merely "an" awareness. You are the ONLY awareness, the ONLY consciousness in existence.

What makes you unique as a so-called "individual" is not your physical attributes, because as we've already pointed out, your body is really a fictional character created by sensory distortions and limitations. In other words, your appearance in physical form is like an old-time magician's trick using "smoke and mirrors" to deceive an audience into seeing something that isn't really there. What you think of as yourself has a lot in common with those self-generated characters you create in your dreams.

You are the sum total of all of your thoughts, emotions, beliefs, experiences, memories, passions and personality traits. Imagine that the energy of all your thoughts, emotions, memories and experiences from the moment you were born until today were collected into a glowing sphere of multicolored energy. That energy form is unique. It vibrates at a frequency and "color" that is unlike anyone who has ever existed. THAT image describes you far more accurately than the unshaven, sleepy-eyed reflection in your bathroom mirror.

DANGER! Explosive Words

Words like God, religion, spirituality, worship, sin, righteousness, etc., are "loaded" insofar as people have strong beliefs and feelings in connection with them. Who can deny that much blood has been spilled over religious differences? You will notice that my books handle religious topics as if I was trying to defuse a bomb! Should I cut the red wire or the blue? To use another analogy, it is sometimes difficult to move through a crowd without rubbing someone the wrong way. Still, I do OK, I guess.

The concept of I AM has been stated in many different ways by many different people. In my view, this is a good thing since it helps the greatest number of people to conceptualize it in a manner that suits them. This is also why I believe that religion serves an important function for certain people. Although I do not personally endorse one religion over another, it is obvious that some folks are comfortable embracing spirituality in a religious group worship context.

In most cases, organized religion presents divinity as outside, above and beyond human beings. In some religions, a mediator or intercessor is required in order for the common man or woman to contact God since, in that religion, humans are considered to be too lowly, sinful or fragile to approach God directly.

God in YOU

What follows are several expressions of the concept of God, I AM, divinity, (fill in the appellation of your choice,) that are not based on an external deity.

"Everything in the universe is within you. Ask all from yourself."

~Rumi

"I am in you and you in me."

~William Blake

"It is not possible that you could ever find yourself anywhere where God was not fully present."

~Emmet Fox

"You are one thing only. You are a Divine Being. An all-powerful Creator. You are a Deity in jeans and a t-shirt, and within you dwells the infinite wisdom of the ages and the sacred creative force of All that is, will be and ever was."

~Anthon St. Maarten

In the Quran at Surah 57, verse 3, speaking of The ONEness of God, it says, "He is the First and the Last, the Evident and the Immanent."

In the Bible, at Revelation 22:13, there is an almost identical text, "I am the Alpha and the Omega, the First and the Last, the Beginning and the End."

Once again, let me remind you that all quotations from so-called Holy books and religious texts are here simply to illustrate that the concept of ONE awareness or Cosmic Consciousness has been in mankind's literature for thousands of years. The ultimate goal of these Keys Of Power publications is to help everyone to better understand how spiritual truths empower us to change our lives in practical mundane ways. Please do not forget that the word "spiritual" is not the same as the word "religious" and although some people have trouble separating the two concepts, they are rather different.

The expression I AM or I AM That I AM is simply a declaration that says, "I exist." It is a statement of BEING. Now in this life, you can be unsure about many things, but when you say I AM, you know it is true. This requires no faith on your part. You don't believe you exist because somebody told you so, or because you read about it somewhere, but because I AM is the one self-evident and undeniable truth. It is the one thing of which there can be no doubt. In fact, at the risk of getting ahead of myself, THIS unquestionable truth is the foundation upon which you will build total confidence and faith to create your world in your image.

I AM The Reader And The Writer

In order for us to fully understand the extent of our power to change the circumstances of our life, we need another critical piece of the puzzle, and it is as follows:

Although our senses give us an impression of a world wherein there are billions of others, individuals outside and all around us, the truth is that of all the people that appear to be around you, you cannot point to anyone else and say I AM. In YOUR world, there is but one I AM and that is YOU. At the risk of making your head spin or your eyebrow raise up Spock-like, it is also equally true that I AM is also the one writing the words you are reading. In my reality, there is but one I AM and that is ME.

If you're scratching your head and a little confused, that is perfectly normal. What will become clearer is precisely how and why knowing this stuff empowers you in amazing ways to create or recreate your life in any way you wish. As I promised from the beginning of this series, in time you will see this knowledge in practical application. Once you see how this works for you, you will feel a great joy, a delightful exhilaration. Your conception of self, of who and what you are, will be changed forever. You will know that you are not merely a being but rather that you are BEING itself, the one and only I AM and infinitely greater than your puny sense organs ever lead you to believe.

"And This Is Practical How?"

Let's step away from the esoteric side of our discussion and begin with a very familiar scenario in which we can see how a change in self-concept can be used to practical advantage in everyday life.

Suppose you are unhappy at your job or maybe you just want more recognition and a promotion. How would you use the principles of the I AM to create a better situation?

Years ago, before I decided to employ myself, I worked in the corporate world and I had occasion to use these principles myself, so I know for sure that they work in the real world. They will work for you as well, provided you carefully follow the method described in the next chapter.

Chapter 9

LET'S GET PRACTICAL

Let's recap the basics:

1) Our anchor to reality resides within the phrase, "I AM That I AM." Although this phrase is found in the Bible, it is more than a religious principle. It is a universal, spiritual, metaphysical principle.

2) The beliefs you accept as true will either imprison or empower you, so choose wisely.

3) Beliefs do NOT have to be "factual" in order to empower you to achieve more than ever before.

3) "I AM" is your core identity. "I AM" is also God's name.

4) Your sense organs give you a severely distorted, false perception of reality.

5) Although our senses make it appear so, the world outside of us and everyone in it is actually not outside but INSIDE of our consciousness!

6) I AM is the quintessential declaration of BEING. It is your core truth and the one thing you can be totally sure of.

7) Great minds have expressed the idea of I AM from many different perspectives: religious, secular, philosophical, and metaphysical.

The Bottom Line

It all boils down to this: I AM is you, your true Self. I AM is GOD. You are God and God is you.

Some people will reject this statement out of hand without even a second thought. In all likelihood, these individuals will assume the very idea is ridiculous or even blasphemous. That is an understandable reaction given the conventional concept of a God outside and separate from us.

To be perfectly honest, I myself grew up in a Christian family and even saying the words "I am God" would have been considered a sin of no small significance. So I truly do understand why some people would have a serious problem with this. In time, you may be able to update your viewpoint enough to see that the concept of the God within is not as ridiculous as it may appear to be at first light.

Practical Application

Now you and I have come to a crossroads. Ahead of you stretches the road less traveled. It is the road to a new and exciting life. This is a happy place that you yourself will call into existence. It is the place where you are free to know yourself, to find your path and to live your life. It is by far a more genuine and powerful way of living.

So, without further ado, let's get to the practical application. For the moment, we are going to put aside the esoteric discussion and focus on a real-world scenario you will have no trouble relating to.

At the end of the last chapter, I posed the following question: Suppose you are unhappy at your job or maybe you just want more recognition and a promotion. How would you use the principles of the I AM to create a better situation?

Some years ago, I found myself in precisely that position. Let me take a few moments to share with you what I did and the results I got. Working in the corporate world was never something that appealed to me. To be perfectly honest with you, I was miserable at my job. My feeling was that this mega-corp didn't appreciate how hard I worked. Neither did they appreciate my potential. As best I could tell, they didn't care if I lived or died.

That was my perception, mind you, not necessarily the reality. Nevertheless, I took that harsh feeling to work with me each day. Have you ever found yourself in a similar situation? It isn't a very nice way to live considering the many hours most of us spend working. It wasn't just my opinion, though. My fellow workers had similar complaints.

Of course, my being in that position at a job I hated was entirely unnecessary. I had temporarily forgotten the teachings of the great masters of my youth. No doubt they would have considered it to be the height of foolishness to expect changes in the outside world without first changing the true reality within.

My choice was simple: either leave my job or stay at my job. One day, a third choice occurred to me. I made the choice to put the spiritual knowledge I had gained over the years into PRACTICAL use. My task was to create changes in the OUTSIDE world by creating changes on the INSIDE world. The "outside" must reflect the inside because the outside IS the inside. That is the Law.

Here's exactly what I did and it could serve as a pattern

you can use if you should decide to do so: One fine morning, I woke up and with as much feeling and enthusiasm as I could muster I declared to myself, "I have a terrific job!" Then I told myself, "My paycheck proves that this company values me because no successful business gives away money without good reason." "I have a terrific job" was followed by, "I AM a valued employee."

Having used these new thoughts and feelings to create a new situation in universal MIND, I now turned my attention to my bosses. Evidently, these people had the secret of success in this company, so the smart move was for me to learn from them. That very day I asked to speak with a manager. Not just any manager, mind you. I made up my mind to talk with the one who I thought liked me the very least! I told him that I admired him and his professional expertise. (This wasn't a lie. He was obviously a good manager, it just didn't appear that he had any fondness for the likes of me!) I told him that I would greatly appreciate it if he would mentor me and teach me everything he could. Although this man never broke a smile to me in the past, his attitude and demeanor changed right before my eyes. He suddenly perked up and agreed to help me. I did likewise with other managers.

My "new reality" included looking at my duties at work "as if" I was already a manager, instead of one of the rank and file employees. In every way I could think of, I made a conscious effort to change my own belief system regarding that job. I looked at the smallest perks of working there as though they were daily blessings. This required some imagination. The objective was to make a fundamental and intentional mental/emotional shift. Remember, I hated this job! So, each day I somehow managed to create in my mind a vision of a job I loved. I held to that vision and it, consequently, altered my words and actions at work.

Change Yourself And Change The World

As you might imagine, there were times that I felt as though I was lying to myself about how great my job was. I had to deny the evidence of my senses and declare with the full might and authority of the I AM presence that this was the best job of my life so far. I knew that there was a spiritual reality that has a direct connection to the material world and that I had the authority to change the outside world by changing the world inside ME. Many thanks to my dad and to the spiritual masters who must have been looking down on me with smiling faces!

So, what was the result of all this crazy New Age mumbo jumbo? To make a long story short, within 30 days of my declaring a new reality in the power of I AM, I was given a "top employee" award - which I received to the applause of the entire assembled staff. This after being at this company for years without any official recognition whatsoever. But wait, there's more, as they say on TV! Within the next couple of months, I was promoted. Somehow, I now found myself as part of the management staff! Naturally, my pay took a hefty upswing. My new position had more and better benefits. I had the respect of the entire staff of over 100 people at my location, who now looked to me as one of their bosses.

The highlight of that season was that this terrific company organized a day-long fishing trip - managers only, of course. Imagine that! I was receiving full pay to enjoy a day on the high seas on a fishing boat chartered exclusively for us. By way of full disclosure, I didn't catch a damn thing that day, but I will never forget driving home that evening and thinking about the awesome power of God within.

QUMRAN TAJ

Chapter 10

HARD WAY VS EASY WAY

The truth of I AM is eternal and unalterable. It is possible to ignore reality or think it ridiculous, but it will always come to light in due course.

If you have reached this 10th chapter, you know that the principle of I AM or I AM That I AM is all about a very real truth, but one that cannot be detected using the basic five human senses. Spiritual, intangible truth is as real as any solid object. To be more accurate, spiritual truth is so real that it literally formats and produces the experiences we all have in the material world. In that respect, those of us who live our lives based on the reality of spirit or the I AM can attest to the fact that a spiritual truth is MORE real than that which our senses report.

You might be thinking, "Well that's only your opinion. Such a thing cannot be proven." If you find yourself having such thoughts, I will reply that you are quite correct. It is impossible for me to prove any of this to you. You can, however, prove it to yourself, if you apply what is contained on these pages.

It can be difficult for someone, particularly someone raised in a western society, as I was, to grasp the concept of an intangible reality. From birth onward, we are taught that things we can taste, touch, smell, hear and see are real. In fact, we believe these tangibles are the MOST real things of all. On the other hand, that which one cannot experience in a tactile, tangible way, particularly mental, emotional, ephemeral or imaginal experiences, tend to be perceived as less than real. It is common to hear people say, "Oh, don't worry yourself about that. It's only your imagination" or "It's all in your head," as if what's in your head is less real than a flower, a stone or a chair.

Why not allow yourself the luxury to suspend judgment for a brief moment to consider an alternative world view? As an alternative to the common wisdom of a solid, material reality, what if the exact opposite were true? What if it is actually the non-physical, or what I like to call spiritual energies, that are the real movers and shakers of our world? What if we discover that by manipulating our spiritual selves, what we think, feel and believe, we automatically cause changes to happen in the world around us?

If that is true, then we have to admit that working with the spiritual root cause of mundane circumstances is a far superior way to get things done. It's like a doctor who treats the cause of illness instead of the symptoms. To follow this analogy, most folks struggle to control the symptoms of their problems instead of working with the root causes of what ails them.

Sadly, most people labor under a false premise. They look outwardly to effect change in their lives, using whatever tools they have at hand. Their sense organs report to them a world that is largely beyond their reach. With such a severely diminished concept of Self, it is no wonder that so many people despair and give up on ever being happy or successful. It becomes for them a futile struggle of "me against the world."

Please do not misunderstand. I am NOT suggesting that you quit your job and spend the rest of your days in a cave seated in a meditative lotus posture waiting for the world to do your bidding! To the contrary, physical activity is a blessing and to engage in meaningful work as a productive member of society is a privilege. A fully self-realized person embraces work as a form of personal mastery. Using spiritual treatment should go hand in hand with the work of your hands toward the fulfillment of your goals.

After a lifetime of using difficult, uncertain methods to get the things you want, this NEW approach may strike you as being strange, impractical or even foolish. You can rest assured that I won't try to change what you believe one way or another. Actually, I am convinced that as a sovereign BEING, you have every right to accept or reject anything you wish. Believe whatever you wish.

You should know, however, that what is contained in these pages are not mere theories or popular notions that happen to be en vogue. Neither are they ideas of my own invention. I do not believe them because of something I read or because someone told me so. Likewise, if you practice the truth contained herein consistently and intelligently, you will get results and judge for yourself the wisdom that the Keys Of Power wish to pass on to you.

Chapter 11

THE RING OF TRUTH

Does not something about this message ring true? It speaks to a part of you that sees itself in these words. The higher self, the TRUE self, the DIVINE ONE calls to itself and you have answered. Otherwise, why are you still reading?

This 11th chapter is a turning point. The balance of this book is rather to the point and the pace quickens. The previous 10 chapters are something of a prelude.

I could have included my own personal experiences with I AM That I AM or related many testimonials from people who have found this message and in the process, they found themselves. What is important is not where I am on my path and how I got here but where you are on yours.

A little personal background might help you understand why it is better for you to walk the path of personal evolution yourself than to have someone tell you about it.

Finding The Masters

In chapter two, I alluded to my father and how he encouraged my brother and me to be avid readers. He was a voracious reader of self-help and self-actualization books and anything he considered to be of practical value. He instilled in us a love of learning and was quick to share the highlights of some fascinating tidbit he picked up in his travels. A healthy curiosity and a thirst for knowledge were great gifts to us.

There were wonderfully inspiring stories and first-hand accounts of people who developed amazing powers and skills to reach their goals using one method or another. There was a series of books that I enjoyed tremendously called "The Life and Teachings of the Masters of the Far East," by Baird T. Spaulding. There was also a book called "Message of a Master," by John McDonald. I read many wonderful books in those days and they served me well on my journey, but these two authors, in particular, captured my imagination in a very powerful way.

Here's the problem I ran into and it is the reason you won't find testimonial stories in this particular volume. While I always wanted to believe that the people in those books really existed and that they had discovered the ancient Keys of Power, I was also plagued with doubt. I remember poring over these wonderful stories and savoring every word, but the question I could never escape was this: what if these stories and the people in them were exaggerated, or even worse, what if my favorite characters were a total fiction created by a clever author? I later learned that the author of my favorite series of books, Baird T. Spaulding, had a reputation for shamelessly embellishing the facts. Still, what I read in his books had a curious ring of truth to it despite discovering that he may have woven truth into a fictional story and claimed it to be a factual account of his experiences.

I finally decided that there was no way I could ever be 100% sure if what I read was fact or fiction, or if it was a mix of the two, or exactly where truth left off in the narrative and fairytale began. It eventually dawned on me that there was ONLY one way to be sure that the spiritual realm and the wondrous powers people were said to have in those books were real. The only way for ME to be sure was to develop some of these powers myself and use them first-hand. Then, and ONLY then, could I be sure that what I had read was not bogus. This is the reason why several times in this series you've been encouraged to try these teachings for yourself and prove them to yourself. Then you will truly know that what I teach you is not only partly true, but completely true and 100% accurate.

For the remaining chapters of this volume one in the Keys Of Power series of books, I will relate the teachings and messages to you faithfully and truthfully, but I offer no proof. Neither do I ask you to believe me. It is suggested that you dwell upon these concepts until they begin to make sense to you. In due course, you may even wonder how something so fundamentally true escaped your notice for all these years! If you want proof of my word, you shall have it once you accept what is being told and you put it into practice in your own life.

'In The Beginning'

Let us begin at the beginning.

In all reality, there is but one BEING, one consciousness, one awareness. There is no other. There is but one who can declare "I AM." That BEING is the ONE reading this program. That BEING is the ONE writing this program.

Although your senses report to your brain that there are many other individuals in the world, this is a false notion. In actual truth, the world, everyone and everything in it, is a projection of the I AM to create a fascinating theatrical drama wherein many apparently separate and distinct characters play their parts.

The real truth is that you are the ONLY BEING in existence. This statement does not suggest an egotistical interpretation, as if you, the reader, are superior to anyone else. Rather, it simply states the unalterable truth that there IS nobody else to be superior to. There is only the eternal BEING that declares I AM That I AM.

So where do we go from here? When once you become aware of your true nature and begin to create from the awareness of I AM That I AM, then manifesting what you desire becomes a case of moving within the Self, using the only creative power there is. Instead of reaching beyond to a fictional sense-based outside world, you will affect changes and new manifestations moving from the source and center of creation. You will go from a struggle and strain approach to changing your environment to a method that flows smoothly and is certain to achieve whatever it is you declare to be so.

Does this strike a chord within you? Do you have an inner sense that truth is to be found somewhere in this direction? In the final chapters, I will take you step by step into the time-tested ways of working from your core, your SOURCE, the awareness, the consciousness of I AM That I AM.

QUMRAN TAJ

Chapter 12

MR. PLAY-DOH

What does the word "God" mean to you? Those of you who have had a religious upbringing like mine tend to imagine God as a bearded man in long white robes sitting on a throne somewhere in heaven high above and far, far away from us. Naturally, other faiths have various concepts of deity.

Please accept my apologies for the limitations of the English language in this respect: My gender-specific references to God as a "He" is due to the fact that English has no appropriate word for a sentient being that is neither male nor female. "He" was chosen simply because it is traditional in my part of the world to refer to God as "He" in the same way one might refer to a boat as "she." No offense is intended to anyone who might erroneously see this practice as gender bias or who may prefer to call God "She."

It should also be noted that the mainstream Abrahamic faiths have tried to distinguish their deity as being uniquely superior to all others by using a capitalized "God" or "Allah," as if these were proper names (they aren't) or as if theirs were the one and only true and supreme God above all others. My use of the capital is merely in deference to a common custom. As should be very obvious to the reader by now, I do not conform to a traditional conception of God, god, goddess or gods!

Beyond Religion

Much innocent blood has been shed quarreling about whose god is the "true" god and what religion is the "right" religion. To me it looks like children fighting in a school yard, pointless and infantile. If only people would look inwardly for the divine, instead of searching outside of themselves. God speaks inside of you with the power and authority to remake and revitalize your life and circumstances.

So, are we talking about some New Age religion here? No, not at all. The I AM That I AM, that is to say, the God within you, is not about religion at all. In fact, let this point be perfectly clear: In this series, whenever I use the word "God," do not imagine I am referring to conventional notions of God and religion. The God I speak of is I AM That I AM, that is to say, the BEING that speaks whenever you or I declare I AM.

Maybe the hardest thing for most people to accept is this

concept of the supreme BEING that not only exists within you, but a supreme BEING that actually IS you.

Let's be brutally honest here, folks. On the surface of it, the very notion that humans and God are one and the same thing is ridiculous on a grand scale. It doesn't make any sense, does it?

For example, ask me what is happening this very moment in the life of a total stranger half way around the world. I have no clue. Ask me why I poured salt into my coffee instead of sugar. I don't know. It was a mistake. One of many mistakes I make every day. Ask me why I invested money in a company whose shares then proceeded to lose value instead of gain value? Obviously, had this been known to me beforehand, I would have made another choice. If I'm really the supreme BEING, why will this body of mine eventually grow old and die?

I could go on asking sensible questions and none of the answers to those questions would suggest that I am God in the flesh. There is yet another problem with the "I am God" pronouncement.

If I say that I am God, what does that make you? When I say I am God does that mean I am YOUR God? Should I expect you to worship me? Are we really trying to say that one human being is God and all the rest are not? Obviously, we are not saying that. Not even close.

The Great Master of Disguise

The concept of the supreme being dwelling within everything and everyone is an extremely ancient philosophy. It is also true that some of the greatest minds throughout the ages and right up to our own era believe that not only is this concept not blasphemy, it is rather logical and intelligent, not to mention being in lockstep with the latest research in quantum physics.

It occurred to me that it might be very helpful to offer a simple analogy or illustration to make sense of what might otherwise be a bit difficult to explain.

Here goes:

We all played make believe games as children. Do you remember Play-Doh? It is colorful modeling clay made for young children. It's great fun to play with!

I remember as a child I would rip off a hunk of Play-Doh and form it into a dinosaur. Out of the same lump of clay, I ripped off another piece and made that one into a man and still another piece became a car or a cat or ANYTHING I wanted. There is no limit to what you can make from this stuff! I can't tell you how many hours of pleasure it gave me to indulge my imagination in this way. Afterward, I'd smoosh them all back into the big lump and start all over again, and again and again.

At one of my workshops not too long ago, I handed out Play-Doh modeling clay to everyone in the audience and told them to shape it into anything they liked. Every single person in the audience was transformed into a child before my very eyes, or so it seemed to me. They slipped into a silent reverie and made these beautifully detailed creations. When they handed them back every item was different but all made from the same thing.

Let's imagine that the Play-Doh in our analogy here is the mysterious stuff from which all things are made. Literally the building blocks of matter itself. This mysterious "stuff" can be shaped into any form the mind can conceive. Now let us call this mysterious substance, this clay, let's call it God. The dinosaur is God, the man is God, the car is God, the cat is God. In short, EVERYTHING is made from the same substance, the same primordial energy, the same fundamental essence we call Play-Doh, also known as "God."

Our analogy needs one more element to be of real service to us. In the beginning, the creative element we are calling God for the purpose of this illustration couldn't go to a store to buy cosmic Play-Doh to make all that is created. No such OTHER anything existed! Instead, God made "all that is" from himself by BECOMING whatever he created. In our illustration, the creator is Play-Doh and from himself, he created the dinosaur, the man, the car, the cat and EVERYTHING that was made. Hence "I AM... That (dinosaur, man, cat, car, etc.)... I AM.

An Inevitable Epiphany

Now God, being a self-aware BEING and making all things from himself, decides to form a BEING that is also self-aware. After all, making objects that don't talk or do much of anything isn't nearly as much fun as pretending to interact with another self-aware being. God decided to make from his own essence a new thing. For the moment, let us call this newly created BEING Mr. Play-Doh. Mr. Play-Doh is a smart guy and after a great deal of deep meditation and introspection, a magnificent thought occurs to him. He is so excited he dashes out of his Play-Doh house, down his Play-Doh driveway to his Play-Doh street lined with Play-Doh trees and Play-Doh people walking their Play-Doh dogs. Surveying everything around him, Mr. Play-Doh makes his grand pronouncement: "I AM Play-Doh!" Or in other words, "I AM God"

Mr. Play-Doh doesn't stop there. He goes and tells his best friend about this marvelous epiphany. After he does, Mr. Play-Doh notices that his Play-Doh friend has an odd expression on his face. So, his friend says, a little ticked, "Well, who died and made YOU God!!?" Mr. Play-Doh replies, "No, NO! You don't understand. It's not just me. YOU are God, too. In fact, EVERYTHING is God."

Well, his friends and neighbors need more time to let this new idea sink in some more. In the meanwhile, Mr. Play-Doh understands that being God also means that, like God, he too has the power to form things from himself just like God does. He knows this for sure because he discovered that he and God are one and the same thing. This begins a glorious journey of self-discovery for Mr. Play-Doh.

Play Your Role Like A True Thespian!

You see, my friends, since you find yourself in the form of a man or a woman, you will display all the limitations of the character that you are playing in this life. You appear to forget things, you make mistakes every day, you have unforeseen accidents, and once you are done, your true essence, God, the only BEING in existence, Cosmic Consciousness, Life Force, Universal Source Power or whatever name you choose to call yourself, smooshes the fictional "you" back into our proverbial lump and makes something new and exciting! Due to the temporary ignorance that is intentionally built into the character you are currently playing, you have been erroneously calling your own divine recycling process "death."

Not to put too fine a point on it, but in actual truth, since God cannot ever die, neither can you. You can retire your character role and exit stage left, but you never die, although some of you will put on a masterful death scene performance! You simply go on to some other role of your choosing. There is no life after death. There is only life after life. What can I say, folks? It's good to be God!

QUMRAN TAJ

Chapter 13

THE TOOL BOX

There is so much more to learn, but what is contained in these pages is sufficient to remake a life. If you embrace the teachings in these books, you will rediscover a power you have always had. You create things. All sorts of things. You can't help yourself really. It is your nature to BE. BEING becomes things. That is its nature. That is your nature. What you become is up to you.

Henceforth, you will create with power and intention. You will set and achieve goals with confidence in the outcome. In a very real sense, you will know the end from the beginning, the alpha and the omega, the beginning and the end.

You will gradually shed your artificially diminished self-concept. Nevertheless, the role you have chosen is a human one. This role doesn't usually include absolute omnipotence with the snap of fingers! Still, your ability to accomplish wonderful things and manifest your most cherished dreams will be limited only by your ability to believe in and apply the law of the I AM That I AM.

Will You Miss The Point?

There is no qualitative difference between you and the divinity called God. The precious knowledge you hold in your hands makes you a god who walks among men. Will you feel superior to others? If you do, you have missed the point entirely. Remember the analogy of Mr. Play-Doh? God isn't just you. God is ALL and ALL is God. How does one manage to feel superior to oneself? Such a person would be deluding themselves and the knowledge of God is not in them.

Should you ever find yourself lording it over others with a swelled head, you may rest assured that you are still playing the part of a weak individual with delusions of grandeur and not the I AM That I AM.

The Basics

The brief statements that follow are set in simple terms. The truth is not made more potent by couching it in high-brow dissertations.

1) You are already a powerful creator.

That's something you have been doing since birth naturally and effortlessly. There's really nothing you need to learn on that score.

You say you don't FEEL powerful? That is to be expected. Why? Because you have wielded that power in a haphazard, unintentional, uncontrolled, misguided and sometimes self-destructive way. Is it any wonder that some lives resemble a train wreck?

May I be blunt here? Since most folks don't know what they're doing, instead of creating a lovely landscape masterpiece, they've turned their lives into an abstract mishmash of shapes that looks like something Picasso would paint!

Weeping Woman by Pablo Picasso

Yes, you do create your environment, but learning to manage your creative power to manifest specifically what you want is the key. We can all agree that creating a life characterized by chaos is something none of us want. Yet, that is precisely what many people DO. Sadly, many of us are victimized and terrified by their own creations.

The Question Is WHAT, Not HOW

So, what do you need to do differently? The answer is simple: Nothing. You don't need to change HOW you're creating your environment. You've been doing a masterful job of that already. You may want to change WHAT you're creating, however. That is an entirely different matter.

Fortunately for all of us, the ways and means to do this are simple and straightforward. You will be working with the very same tools you have been using rather successfully all of your life. There's not much of a learning curve here. The only difference now will be WHAT you create, not how you create it.

The master tools required for this task are all familiar to you. They cause creative energy to flow from your inner reality to your so-called outer reality.

They are as follows:

1) Your thoughts.

These thoughts have power, but they must be infused with an even more intense energy that fills thought forms with a dynamic substance. What is that "dynamic substance?" See number 2.

2) Feelings. The more intense and focused the emotion, the better.

If you think of your thoughts as a cake mold, the cake batter you pour into that mold can be likened to the intense feelings you pour into your thought forms. Both cake batter and the feelings you dwell upon will harden into real experiences.

3) Beliefs or internal "programming."

Your thoughts and feelings must pass through the filter of your belief system. It is this Triad of Creation that determines what you will actually do and say in this world and those actions will, in turn, have their own repercussions. Beliefs also influence how long it will take for manifestation into the world of the senses.

For instance, if you are convinced that you can't do, have or be a certain thing, you will be working at cross purposes to your own desire and progress will be slower. If your belief system denies it or believes your goal is too difficult to achieve or that it will take a very long time to realize, it will telescope the manifestation farther into the future.

Now let's be clear on this one point: extending the time it takes to manifest does NOT mean it will never manifest. The Law is, any thought or emotion held in any mind long enough MUST manifest in some appropriate way.

This is why it is so important to create beliefs that empower you, not disempower you.

Many people have tried to apply the principles of the Law of Attraction but failed to get the results they wanted. Deep-seated beliefs undermine their efforts and after getting little or no results, they return to old habits that give them the same old results they have always gotten. Had they persisted in their creative activity, results would have come sooner or later. These individuals end up believing either the Law of Attraction doesn't work or that it doesn't work for them.

Changing Subconscious Beliefs

The question of how to change one's beliefs, especially those stuck in the subconscious mind, is one of the most common questions my students ask during workshops and classes.

Never forget that you have the power to replace disempowering beliefs. Fortunately, you don't need to be a psychologist or even an expert on how the subconscious mind works in order to create a healthy belief system.

Keys To Subconscious Power

The subconscious mind...

1) Cannot tell the difference between a real experience and an experience that is vividly imagined.

That, my friends, is a fact of such critical importance that I will repeat it for emphasis: the subconscious mind cannot tell the difference between a real experience and an experience that is vividly imagined.

This simple fact gives you almost carte blanche to reformatting your beliefs about virtually EVERYTHING! In the hands of an intelligent reader, this knowledge is more valuable than pure gold.

2) Is only aware of the "now" moment. In other words, any statement on your part, any affirmation, any declaration that you want the subconscious mind to believe and act upon must be stated as if it is already true here and now. The subconscious mind knows only now.

Let us recap:

1) You are already a powerful creator.

2) Three Keys of Power: a) Thoughts b) Emotions c) Beliefs.

3) The name "I Am That I AM," the name of God, can be broken down into three parts:

1) "I AM" - the ultimate declaration of BEING.

2) "That" refers to whatever the I AM, the God that is you, chooses to become or form itself into.
3) "I AM" is the declaration that I AM all that is, all that was and all that will be. It is an exultation of success. It is the closing parenthesis that includes everything between the opening and closing parentheses. It is the eternal cycle that goes from Source to manifestation and returns again to Source. It is the declaration that God is all and all is God.

Essential Power Steps

So, with this perspective in mind, let us get back to the question of how we create our environment purposely while simultaneously replacing negative beliefs with positive ones.

In can be stated this way:

a) In your mind and imagination, you actually create situations, circumstances, and realities. To make something happen, it is critically important to blend thoughts and feelings together so that they are pointed to the same goal.

b) You must then experience what you want as clearly and vividly as possible INSIDE of you AS IF the object of your desire exists in full form HERE and NOW.

It is at this precise juncture that many folks go astray and yet it is this very step in the process that can make the difference between getting what you want or not. Ignore this at your peril.

It is not enough to see your dream home, car, loved one or job from an outside perspective as if looking at a photograph. You must BE in the picture yourself! If you envision a new home, then see yourself in the kitchen preparing dinner or entertaining guests or lounging on the patio. If there is a specific neighborhood you imagine your house is located in, then visit that area. Learn everything there is to know about the schools, businesses, and nearby attractions. LIVE in your "new" situation to the extent possible or practical.

Enhanced Imagination

Your master key to success here is imagination. Some of my students have told me they have difficulty visualizing things. The good news is that there are many ways to supercharge your imagination.

When people think of the word "imagination," they typically think of one's ability to create mental images. That might be all that is needed for an artist painting a scene on canvas, for example. For our purposes, ideally you want to bring as many of your five basic senses into play as possible: sight, hearing, touch, smell or whatever is pertinent to the goal.

"I tell you I don't visualize well and now you want me to add other senses!?" That might be a natural reaction to what I just suggested, but not to worry, my friend. Permit me to remind you that you are ALREADY successfully creating your environment. You are already doing a great job of manifesting ... even if you haven't been aware of doing so.

The thing to remember is that you naturally include your other senses in everyday visualizations without thinking of it as such. It is mentioned here because whereas everyone creates as a matter of habit, you may not be consciously aware of your own creative process in all the particulars. In planning a new project, you may overlook the other ways and means you use to make a thing real to you. If pure visualization is not your strong suit, please feel free to bring any and all other senses to the party!

Recliner Lust

Let's illustrate this process with a very mundane object. You're at the shopping mall and see a beautiful leather recliner. Instantly, you are in love! Then you catch sight of the price tag and instantly, your heart is broken! It is more money than you have ever spent on a piece of furniture.

You decide you will manifest this as the powerful creator that you are. How exactly should you go about this? Let's take this step by step:

1) Enter the store.

2) Sit in the chair. Close your eyes and feel your weight sink into the cushions. Touch the leather. Is it smooth, or does it have a texture? Is it cool to the touch? Does the recliner have a certain smell? What did it sound like when you sat in it? Be sure to commit every sensation to memory.

3) Ask the salesperson for a brochure with pictures and the description of the piece. Take a sample swatch of the leather it is made from, if it is available.

4) Go home and pick a spot the chair will occupy.

5) Using your memory of the experience at the store, imagine sitting in the chair again except now, see the room as it will appear when your recliner is located in the spot you've picked out.

6) Imagine your every emotion, from the first sight of the delivery truck coming to your home to the men carrying it through your door and your signing their proof of delivery receipt.

7) Feel the joy of owning this beautiful piece of furniture! Imagine your friends and family fawning over it and commenting on how luxurious it looks. Feel yourself brimming with pride.

Keep repeating this procedure and enjoy it as you would a daydream. There should be no struggle or strain to this activity. In fact, any such effort would be counterproductive. Just have fun! Do this frequently until the recliner is in your home. Do not be concerned about how it will arrive or if you can afford the staggering ticket price. Simply live it in your creative reality until it sits in your house.

As surely as night follows day, you will own that recliner, provided you stick to the process.

Yet Another Recap!

1) You are already God, the I AM That I AM of the world. You do not need lessons on being a creator. You only need to become aware of who you are, what you are, and what you are creating.

2) A simple way to think about the creative method is the Triad of creation: Thoughts ~ Feelings ~ Beliefs. Make sure you direct them in positive ways to specific results.

3) You are just as capable of successfully creating negative results as positive ones. The choice is yours.

You've Got The Tools, Now What?

Well, that's a mighty fine tool box you have there! I see it's filled with just the right equipment for the tasks ahead, but I can see by the expression on your face there's something missing.

Did I forget to tell you that your fancy tools also come with an equally fancy customer support program? Yes, they do. After all, there are many important questions that need answers:

~Are there Karmic consequences to my actions as the I AM?

~How can I gain the wisdom to use my power for good?

~How do the Keys Of Power help me cope with guilt and fear?

~Am I responsible for the sufferings of my loved ones?
~This much power is intimidating. Is it too much for me?
~Does accepting this mean I must leave my religion?

Satisfying, authoritative answers to these and many other important questions are all thoroughly covered in upcoming volumes of the Keys Of Power series.

The road ahead is full of wonderful experiences that will serve you and the world rather well.

Chapter 14

THE CROWN

There are no words in any language to express my emotions as I write this last chapter. After being so profoundly inspired by spiritual masters of long ago, the time is ripe to make my own humble contribution to these teachings. As a boy, my imagination was enthralled with tales of powerful works and the mysterious adepts of a craft I knew nothing of. For some reason I could not fathom at the time, it was extremely important to me to know if these stories were true or not. It was a burning passion that compelled me to cross oceans of time in search of the truth.

Now you have taken my place, reading a book as I did so many years ago. There was no way for me to know back then if the authors of these beloved books were writing fact or fiction masquerading as fact. You may now find yourself in the same quandary, wondering if you can trust the words written here.

For this reason, it gives me much pleasure to finally testify that the teachings found in this book are true and reliable! I write this in all good conscience because these writings are verified as to their accuracy, not based on the opinions and theories of other individuals, but rather based on my own first-hand experience actually applying what I have taught you here.

The personal first-hand confirmations I speak of were not a few scattered instances. To the contrary, using these extraordinary God-powers possessed by all normal human beings has been a way of life for me. In truth, it would be impossible to recount for sheer number the occasions wherein I performed works for myself and others that would be difficult for most readers to believe. No, I do not consider myself to be a spiritual master, per se. I am a normal human being with common frailties and flaws, even as you are. Still, I am convinced that it is humankind's natural domain as the "I AM," pure divine BEING, to function in this way. It is how we are ALL made.

This brings me to the many accounts of miraculous feats performed by people of long ago. My thoughts run to religious books, such as the Bible and other holy texts. Although I was raised as a Christian and serious student of the Bible as the word of God, I have since come to the conclusion that it is a textbook of psychology, metaphysics, and spiritual instruction and a religious text only when religionists use it as such.

To me, it is pointless to debate whether the stories in the Bible should be taken literally or as allegories. Even a purely fictional story can be a true story if it teaches truth unencumbered by so-called "facts." Indeed, it is written in Matthew 13:34 that "Jesus spoke all these things to the crowds in parables. He did not tell them anything without parables." Was Jesus lying to his listeners when he spoke of events and people in parables? Not at all. Were not these fictional tales used to illustrate truths in a way they could be more easily understood?

Taking a step further, what if Jesus only exists in the pages of the Bible? In my view, it does not matter. Jesus lives as the "I AM." As such, he dwells within you and within me. At the risk of earning your disbelief, I confess that I myself have commanded the winds and storms as he did along with other powerful works that some might call miraculous. Since I know that I exist and have performed powerful works myself, it means that even if Jesus was a character written into the Biblical narrative, he is STILL real because I am real. Having said that, please know that what I have done, you may do also and even greater works than these since you and I are the same ONE.

So it is that truth can be gleaned from many sources, both fictitious and factual alike. On the other hand, what I have related to you in this book are NOT parables or truth wrapped within fiction. It is truth spoken in a simple and straightforward way. If you apply these teachings, you will be able to accomplish the most amazing things! I encourage you to read and re-read this information. Then make practical use of it until it becomes second nature to you.

Many spend their lives crying tears of regret, tears of grief, tears of self-pity. The knowledge of the one BEING, the I Am That I Am, empowers us, yes, but it does much more. It frees us on so many levels. It shows us what is real and what is not. It soothes our hurts and reveals the ways and means to a better life.

In the end, the greater our knowledge of our true nature and BEING, the greater our solace and release from unnecessary emotional burdens born of ignorance and delusion. Does this mean we are freed to do what we know to be hateful? Yes and no. We can do harm, as any common criminal might, but harmful acts are ultimately expressions of self-hatred. Since there is truly no other BEING, to strike your brother is to strike yourself. There are painful consequences of hate and malice and, make no mistake, those pains will be visited upon you.

You can go from tears to triumph when you stand forth in the understanding of who and what you truly are. Instead of being the victim of a capricious world, from this very moment you can call into existence a new world wherein you cast off the chains of servitude and reclaim the crown of your birthright.

ABOUT THE AUTHOR

Qumran Taj, or "Q" as most people know him, has spent a lifetime searching for the spiritual truth behind all faiths and philosophies. His journey has taken him down both familiar and fantastic paths. He has been a Christian minister, Pagan high Priest, wizard, spiritual guide, Professional Life Coach, motivational public speaker, published author, and self-empowerment mentor.

Q's articles, poems, and quotations have been published in many respected newspapers, magazines, books, and online. He has been interviewed on television, radio, and for the award-winning feature film documentary/drama The Montauk Chronicles.

Mr. Taj writes, conducts classes, workshops, and lectures on many facets of personal empowerment, self-improvement and how to overcome life's many challenges. Q is also available for private coaching and consultation.

Q lives on the beautiful east end of Long Island, New York. Yeah, it's a tough life but somebody has to live it!

To contact Qumran Taj visit www.KeysOfPower.com or via email at qumran_taj@yahoo.com

QUMRAN TAJ

www.ingramcontent.com/pod-product-compliance
Lightning Source LLC
Chambersburg PA
CBHW042322150426
43192CB00001B/22